Making the Bridegroom's Speech

John Bowden

A How To Book

ROBINSON

ROBINSON

First published in Great Britain in 2000 by How To Books Ltd

This edition published in 2015 by Robinson

Copyright © How To Books Ltd 2000

1 3 5 7 9 10 8 6 4 2

A CIP catalogue record for this book is available from the British Library.

ISBN: 978-1-85703-567-4 (paperback)
ISBN: 978-1-84803-393-1 (ebook)

Cover design by Baseline Arts Ltd, Oxford
Produced for How To Books by Deer Park Productions, Tavistock
Typeset by Pantek Arts Ltd, Maidstone
Printed and bound in Great Britain by Bell & Bain Ltd, Glasgow

Robinson
An imprint of
Little, Brown Book Group
Carmelite House
50 Victoria Embankment
London EC4Y 0DZ

An Hachette UK Company
www.hachette.co.uk

www.littlebrown.co.uk

NOTE: The material contained in this book is set out in good faith for general guidance and no liability can be accepted for loss or expense incurred as a result of relying in particular circumstances on statements made in the book. Laws and regulations are complex and liable to change, and readers should check the current position with relevant authorities before making personal arrangements.

How To Books are published by Robinson, an imprint of Little, Brown Book Group. We welcome proposals from authors who have first-hand experience of their subjects. Please set out the aims of your book, its target market and its suggested contents in an email to Nikki.Read@howtobooks.co.uk

Making the Bridegroom's Speech

Contents

Preface

What is as reliable as rain on a Saturday at Lords, as constant as time and as inevitable as toast falling butter-side down? It's the thousands of bridegrooms-to-be who each year look forward to making their wedding speech with as much relish as they would a visit from the Inland Revenue or an appointment with the dentist.

Fear not, help is at hand! This essential little handbook is written especially and exclusively for the 'trepid' bridegroom. It will show you how to prepare and present a unique, relevant and memorable speech that includes just the right balance of emotion, sincerity and humour. And it will supply you with a rich selection of stories, jokes and quotations you may wish to use or adapt.

Times and manners change, but human nature and the human condition do not. Don't be embarrassed about being emotionally honest and patently sincere. What can make your speech gripping is the potential to *involve* the guests on a subjective level, to make them *empathise* with your deepest feelings and – most importantly – to *forge a bond* between them and you.

John Bowden

For Paula, my bride and joy!

1 Learning the Essentials

*The bridegroom's speech is expected
to be middle-of-the-road.*

In this chapter:

➤ Confirming the programme
➤ Knowing your purpose
➤ Getting the tone right
➤ Remembering the golden rules

As the bridegroom, you are expected to say a few words on the big day. The problem is we don't get much practice, do we? That's why this first chapter gets right back to basics by reminding you, or perhaps telling you for the first time, about the **essential requirements** of any successful bridegroom's speech.

What you must do is make a little speech which shows you understand and appreciate the momentousness of the occasion whilst at the same time keeping all the guests entertained and amused.

The audience is on your side. They are not a jury. They are willing you to do well. And, quite frankly, they won't give a damn if you fluff a line or two. What they *will* mind, though, is if it becomes embarrassingly obvious that you have not even bothered to take the time or effort to find out what is expected of you.

> **?**   **Is this you?**
>
> ➤ I've never spoken in public before. Help!
> ➤ I know I'm supposed to be sensitive and sincere but I'm not sure what message, if any, I'm supposed to convey.
> ➤ I've been told that all I need to say is how I genuinely feel. Is that all there is to it?
> ➤ I want to make a speech that has real impact.
> ➤ What I really need is a simple checklist of do's and don'ts for a bridegroom's speech.

➤1 Confirming the programme

Traditionally, the **bride's father** makes the first speech. He needs to come across as solid, thoughtful and sensible. But he also needs to allow the lighter more humorous side of his personality to shine through.

After the warm up act comes the **bridegroom**. Your contribution is expected to be a little more varied and adventurous.

You need to show you understand the importance and significance of the day, and to thank a lot of people for a lot of things. And you need to do these things in an entertaining, emotional, yet amusing way.

Finally comes the **best man**. His speech should contain plenty of humorous asides and friendly little digs at you, but these should all be underpinned with a few congratulatory thoughts and optimistic remarks about your future.

However, this conventional pattern of speeches is becoming somewhat outdated. For example, it assumes that the bride was brought up by two parents

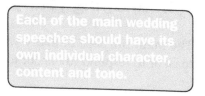

Each of the main wedding speeches should have its own individual character, content and tone.

– and today over two million people in Britain haven't been. And things have changed socially and culturally too – girl power and all that. Today far more women than ever literally want to speak for themselves.

So now it's perfectly acceptable for speeches to be made by other people instead of, or as well as, the traditional big three – perhaps by a **close family friend**, by the **bride's mother**, by the **bride and groom jointly**, or by the **bride** herself. It all depends on the particular circumstances, attitudes and backgrounds of the newlyweds.

The speeches usually begin after the guests have finished eating. Their glasses should be charged *before* anyone speaks. If there is a toastmaster, he will say something like 'Ladies and Gentlemen, pray silence for Mr Ben Nevis who will propose a toast to

Mr Sydney and Mrs Pearl Harbour'. If there is no toast-master, the best man often performs the role, but usually in a less formal manner: 'Ladies and Gentlemen, please be silent as Mr Ben Nevis proposes a toast to Mr Sydney and Mrs Pearl Harbour.'

> The important thing is to find out what the programme of speeches will be and precisely where you will fit into it.

➤ 2 Knowing your purpose

The main purpose of every wedding speech is to propose a toast or to respond to one, or to do both.

➤ **The bride's father (or close family friend, relative or god-father)**: proposes a toast to the bride and groom.

➤ **The bridegroom (possibly with the bride)**: responds to the toast and then proposes a second toast.

➤ **The best man (or best girl)**: responds to the second toast on behalf of the bridesmaids (and any other attendants). He or she may also decide to wind up with a toast to the bride and groom.

➤ 3 Getting the tone right

This is one of the most important days in your life. Your speech should reflect this. It should be:

➤ **Emotional**: You should feel free to display strong personal feelings. Let them see the joy that your bride has brought into your life. However, you must be genuine. False heartiness, cheap sincerity and – worst of all – crocodile tears will all be obvious to an audience.

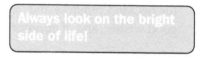

➤ **Optimistic**: This is not the time to share your personal woes, paint a gloomy picture of the present or offer dire predictions about the future. Stress your certainty that you

will have a wonderful life together. Yes, there will be problems, but together you will face them head on and will not be found wanting.

➤ **Enlivened with humour**: Inject a little humour into your speech. You do not need to be a stand-up comedian, indeed you should not be. But you must allow the humorous side of your personality to shine through. Let's face it, when the best man starts to speak, you're going to be the butt of many of his jokes. So take the initiative. Make a preemptive strike. Nothing cruel or unkind though. Just a few friendly put-downs.

➤ 4 Remembering the golden rules

This simple ten-point plan will ensure the contents of your speech will be memorable – and for the right reasons!

➤ Make it clear that you are also speaking on behalf of your new bride – unless she is going to say a few words of her own.

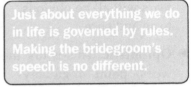

Just about everything we do in life is governed by rules. Making the bridegroom's speech is no different.

➤ Thank the bride's father, or whoever spoke first, for his kind remarks and good wishes, and, if appropriate, for laying on this reception.

➤ Thank your parent(s) for the help and support you have received over the years.

➤ Tell everyone that you are the luckiest man in the world.

➤ Thank everyone for attending – and for their generous presents.

➤ Have a few friendly digs at your best man.

➤ Say a few complimentary words about the bridesmaids before proposing a toast to them.

➤ Learn your opening and closing lines by heart but rehearse the rest of your speech not to be perfect, but to be comfortable. If you feel comfortable, so will your audience.

➤ Try to wrap your speech up within five to ten minutes. Leave them wanting more.

➤ Enjoy the moment!

✓ **Checklist**

Make sure you know the order of speeches.

Don't forget to respond to the first toast and later propose a second toast.

Keep the overall tone of your speech sincere and emotional but lighten it occasionally by targeting some friendly humour against your best man.

Follow the bridegroom's ten golden rules and you won't go far wrong.

2 ► Conveying Your Feelings to the Guests

The most powerful bridge between a speaker and his audience is emotion. When a listener feels the emotion of your words, that listener is hooked.

In this chapter:

➤ Being sincere and emotional
➤ Thanking just about everyone
➤ Weaving in a couple of quotations

Mention sincerity and emotion to many bridegrooms and they roll their eyes. Emotion is soppy. An emotional person cannot watch re-runs of *Sleepless in Seattle*, *Titanic* or *Ghost* without dipping into a box of Kleenex. An emotional person will embarrass you by invading your personal space and hugging you in public.

But things are slowly and quietly changing and you don't need to be a 'new man' to appreciate that emotion is an integral part of every human being. Without it we would be no more than machines. This possibly is the most important day in your life. You should **feel free to display strong personal feelings**. Even the most extravagant emotional outpourings will not sound out of place – so long as they're genuine!

People want more than to just listen to stories, however well they may be told. They also want to experience one or two good, soul-satisfying lingering emotions.

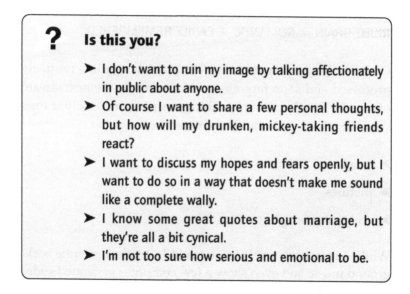

? Is this you?

➤ I don't want to ruin my image by talking affectionately in public about anyone.

➤ Of course I want to share a few personal thoughts, but how will my drunken, mickey-taking friends react?

➤ I want to discuss my hopes and fears openly, but I want to do so in a way that doesn't make me sound like a complete wally.

➤ I know some great quotes about marriage, but they're all a bit cynical.

➤ I'm not too sure how serious and emotional to be.

➤1 Being sincere and emotional

It's all very well saying that you are over the moon, on top of the world, walking on air. The audience may well think 'How nice', but they won't be moved. The trick is not to talk about your feelings, but to **express your emotions** by saying things that will awaken a genuine empathy in your listeners.

Much research has gone into the workings of the human brain. To simplify things grossly, it is divided into hemispheres or halves, each of which is good at different things.

> Put yourself in your audience's shoes. You need to think about the kind of thing that will have a positive effect on them and stick in their memories.

LEFT BRAIN = **L**OGICAL + QUICKLY **L**OST

RIGHT BRAIN = **R**OMANTIC + EASILY **R**EMEMBERED

Ordinary language goes to the left brain, where it is routinely processed and soon forgotten – driven out by the next stream of words. People remember things much more easily if they stimulate the right brain. They remember:

➤ music

➤ pictures

➤ emotional images.

While it may be possible to play a little gentle, romantic background music and even show a few computer-generated slides of you and your bride as you speak, the simplest and most effective way to make your speech engaging and memorable is to use emotion to good effect. As the writer C.S. Forrester reminds us, 'There is no denying the fact that words

> What you must do is take the listener by the hand and guide him or her through your valley of emotions without ever having to mention any of those emotions by name.

spoken from the full heart carry more weight than all the artifices of rhetoric'.

Don't tell them, show them! You need to concentrate, not on the emotion itself, but on the situation that gave rise to it:

> 'It was as if I had seen a vision. She was sitting in the café, alone, or at least I didn't notice anyone else, so dazzled was I by the sight of her. What was her name, where did she live, what sort of life did she lead? I knew nothing about her and I wanted to know everything. What was her favourite colour, did she prefer tea or coffee, what music set her feet tapping? I was overcome by a painful and limitless curiosity.'

Think of your favourite books, music, films. Don't they all share this lingering quality? Too many speakers try to tell too much, and too much of what they tell is not unique. If they drone on interminably about how they spent months shyly observing their beloved as she walked around town, is it really surprising when listeners lose interest and mentally switch off?

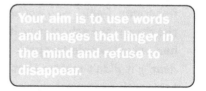

Your aim is to use words and images that linger in the mind and refuse to disappear.

Life is made up of *moments*, pivotal times when something *really* important happens, when you are emotionally hit for six, or when you make a decision that changes the course of your life. Don't bore your listeners with a long build-up or unnecessary explanation. Get straight to the heart of the matter. Focus on a **single pivotal incident** in your life. Provide a snapshot and it will keep the story alive in your audience's mind and heart.

Describe a single, uncomplicated, poignant scene which your audience can visualise. A picture is worth a thousand words.

Paradoxically, the more *apparently* mundane and ordinary the circumstances surrounding the occasion, the more powerful and extraordinary will be the emotions it evokes. The following simple yet memorable scene was created by Paul Wride:

The right mental image can pack a real emotional punch.

> 'It was the most important thing that had ever happened in my life. I had been chosen to play the fisherman, Daniel, who would row his wife, Rachel, across the river in the school play. It didn't matter that Daniel had only six words to speak ("We will soon be there, dear"); it didn't matter that the boat was an upturned table with cardboard stuck to the sides and was pulled jerkily across the stage by four stage hands who could be seen by the entire audience; it didn't matter that the whole play lasted 25 minutes and Daniel was on the stage for less than one. What *did* matter was that Daniel was married to Rachel and Rachel was played by (*bride*) ... And today, 14 years on, Daniel has married Rachel for real!'

➤ **2** Thanking just about everyone

In many ways, a bridegroom's speech can be thought of as a general thank you speech. If it moves, thank it; if it doesn't move, thank it. **Thank anyone and everyone** who has helped make this day so special.

The danger, though, is that your speech can end up sounding like an Oscar-winning acceptance speech.

> It is almost impossible for a bridegroom to overstate his thanks.

The best way to avoid this happening is to lighten all your genuine words of thanks with little touches of humour:

'First of all, I'd like to thank (*bride*) for marrying me. She's the most witty, warm and wonderful woman I know. She does everything for me. She even wrote this speech.

'I'd also like to thank my new father-in-law (*name*) for his kind words. He doesn't know the meaning of the word meanness. Mind you, he doesn't know the meaning of lots of other words either.

'Thanks, too, must go to our mothers for all their help, which was above and beyond the call of duty. My mum's a very responsible lady. If there's a problem it's odds on that she's responsible.

'Thank you all so much for your generous gifts. With all those saucepans and toasters it looks like I'm going to have to get used to boiled toast.

'I'd like to add a word of thanks to my parents for their contribution to today's festivities and for teaching me the difference between right and wrong, so I know which I'm enjoying at any particular time.

'Then I must thank (*name*) for being my best man, though I'm not sure how thankful to be because I haven't heard his speech yet.

'And finally, I must say a word of thanks to the bridesmaids. You did your job magnificently. Obviously I will use you every time I get married from now on.'

➤ 3 Weaving in a couple of quotations

Everyone enjoys hearing a particularly witty or wise turn of phrase or an apt quotation. The **right words** can illuminate your thoughts in a most telling way and really lift your speech. But they must be the right words.

Try to avoid anything remotely negative, sneering or cynical. The problem is, many of the best quotes are negative, sneering or cynical. So if you feel you really must use one or two, reverse them to show this most definitely does *not* apply to you or your new bride:

'Someone once said that a successful marriage involves falling in love many times. I agree, but would add a few words. A successful marriage involves falling in love many times *with the same woman.*'

Quotations are intended to promote smiles and nods rather than a strong emotional reaction or helpless mirth. They may well describe some profound and universal truth, but they are not uniquely relevant to your circumstances and background. Not only that, by definition, they are someone else's words, not your own. For these reasons, they should be spread very thinly, like caviar, not piled on liberally, like marmalade. One or two quotes are plenty for any wedding speech.

Very few quotes will cause a lump in the throat or will be received with a knee-slapping bellylaugh. Their merit usually lies in their encapsulation of a truth, a smart observation or a humorous example.

Quoting people can also sound pompous. Just give a couple of appropriate lines and do it in a very casual way. If you are quoting someone famous, it is a good idea either to make it clear you had to look it up or give the impression you're not absolutely sure of your source:

> 'I am reminded of the words of John Keats – reminded, I should say by Maggie, who looked it up last night ...'

> 'Wasn't it Jane Austen who wrote that ... ?'

> 'I think it was the intellectual giant Katie Price who once said ...'

If you want to quote someone less well known, don't mention him or her by name. If you do, the reaction will probably be an audible 'Who?' Rather, say something like: 'Someone once said ...' or 'It has been said that ...'.

Alternatively, you could attribute the quotation to someone more famous. Oddly enough, this ploy will immediately increase your audience's appreciation of those words of wit and wisdom. But make sure the person you name sounds as if he or she *could* have said that.

> In speechmaking, we work back from Newton's Law that every action has an equal and opposite reaction. We decide the reaction we want and then work back to choose the words that will produce it.

As Woody Allen didn't say, 'The key is to cause an emotional reaction in your audience, not necessarily to be factually accurate.'

Here are just a few quotes on love and marriage, which may or may not be right for your speech. Even if they're not quite in tune with what you're trying to say or how you're trying to say it, at least they should get your little grey cells working on what kind of material would work best for you.

Love is . . .

> 'Love is the wine of existence' (Henry Ward Beecher)

> 'Love is the poetry of the senses' (Honoré de Balzac)

> 'Love is not getting, but giving. It is sacrifice. And sacrifice is glorious!' (Marie Dressler)

Of marriage

> 'There's no greater risk, perhaps, than matrimony, but there's nothing happier than a happy marriage' (Benjamin Disraeli)

'Marriage is our last, best chance to grow up' (Kahlil Gibran)

'Man and wife, a king and queen with one or two subjects, and a few square yards of territory of their own: this, really is marriage. It is true freedom because it is true fulfilment, for man, woman and children' (D.H. Lawrence)

Declarations of love

'O, my luve's like a red, red rose,
That's newly sprung in June:
O, my luve's like a melodie
That's sweetly play'd in tune' (Robbie Burns)

'How do I love thee? Let me count the ways.
I love thee to the depth and breadth and height
My soul can reach ...' (Elizabeth Barrett Browning)

'Will you love me in December as you do in May,
Will you love me in the good old fashioned way?
When my hair has all turned grey,
Will you kiss me then and say,
That you love me in December as you do in May?' (James J. Walker)

✓ **Checklist**

Emotion can make your speech truly absorbing because it is an invisible chain that links person to person, regardless of age, gender, race, background or creed.

Don't forget to thank *everyone* who has helped to make today so special.

Include one or two romantic, humorous or sentimental quotations which seem particularly apt given your personal circumstances and background.

3 Adding a Little Humour

Every successful speech needs an injection of humour.

In this chapter:
➤ Making 'em laugh
➤ Having a friendly dig at your best man
➤ Telling jokes and stories
➤ Rehearsing a few 'ad-lib' lines

A bridegroom's speech should be sincere and emotional and should thank just about everyone for just about everything.

If you sandwich all your emotional outpourings between generous slices of humour, two huge benefits will result. Firstly, you will create a balanced speech that has something for everyone. Secondly, a weighty thought and a good joke will always reinforce each other in a kind of verbal synergy. If a serious message comes immediately after a good laugh, its effect on your audience will be at least doubled.

When it comes to questions of propriety and political correctness, things continually change. Keep up with the times and judge how broadminded your audience is likely to be. If you have any doubts about a joke, cut it. It may be stunningly good in your opinion, but if you offend or embarrass your audience, you will have a hard time winning them over again.

? Is this you?

➤ My new bride's family and my family hardly know each other. How can I create a speech which they will all find relevant, amusing and entertaining?

➤ Is it possible to be both emotional and funny in the same speech?

➤ I'm expecting a little ribbing from one or two people in the audience. It would be useful to have a few lines prepared which I could throw back at them, if this happens.

➤ I know it's traditional for the best man to have a go at the groom, but can the groom take the mickey out of the best man?

➤ Do I need to be 'squeaky clean'?

➤1 Making 'em laugh

Everyone loves a good gag. If you can find a relevant joke you are onto a winner. Matching your choice of material to the nature of the guests is easy when the group all know each other – and they all know you and your bride. At wedding receptions this is often *not* the case, so you must choose your jokes and one-liners with care. You'll find plenty of potential material in Chapter 7.

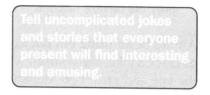

Let's assume your best man, Ian, had a nasty bout of food poisoning while on his hols last year. There is no need to bring all that up again. One simple gag will do the job:

> 'Ian went to Greece last summer ... had the shish kebabs all week.'

Now **everyone** present should find that amusing - with the possible exception of Ian.

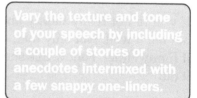

Finally, remember to keep your speech clean – well cleanish anyway. Nobody will be shocked by a little innuendo – in fact, that's expected:

> 'I love (bride) terribly – but I'm sure I'll get better at it.'

> '(Bride) took a Polaroid snap of me in the altogether last week. Then she took the picture out of the camera, looked at it and said, "I'll have to get it enlarged." '

> 'A friend of mine is a born-again Christian. His wedding night was such a disappointment to him. He went into the bedroom and there was his lovely bride in the bed.

"My own love," he said, "I had hoped to find you on your knees at the bedside." "Oh, all right," she said. "But it gives me terrible hiccups." '

Aim to be amusing but not *too* risqué. Before you tell a story or crack a joke, ask yourself whether it passes this test which the late and great Bob Monkhouse devised for all his potential material:

1. Do *you* think it is funny?

2. Can you say it confidently and with comfort?

3. Is there any danger of offending anyone?

4. Will they understand and appreciate it?

Do *you* think it is funny?

If you're not really happy about a joke or a story you will not tell it well. Not only that, the guests probably won't find it funny either. Follow this showbiz adage: If in doubt, leave it out.

Can you say it confidently and with comfort?

Stick to the KISS principle: Keep It Short and Simple. Ask yourself: Is this story right for *me*? A true story about one of your own amusing or embarrassing experiences will have far more effect and novelty value than a repeated old chestnut which some of your audience may have heard before.

Is there any danger of offending anyone?

The traditional advice is to avoid anything racist, sexist or ageist, and steer well clear of politics, religion and disabilities.

The problem is that if you do this automatically many of the best topics for jokes are lost. So use your common sense. Uncle Jack, in his electric wheelchair would prefer to have his leg pulled about the fine he incurred for speeding to get to the wedding on time, than to be ignored altogether.

Will they understand and appreciate it?

Your audience may be aged anywhere between 2 and 92 (nowadays even older) and they will probably have a wide range of backgrounds. So it is impossible to give a speech totally suited to everyone. However, what you can do is avoid extremes of, on the one hand, telling childish jokes and, on the other hand, telling complicated, technical stories comprehensible only to a professor of nuclear physics.

But whatever you do, make sure you never sink to the lavatorial. A speech which consistently aims at the lowest common denominator will not inspire affection or respect, and such a performance is ultimately barren of genuine humour.

➤2 Having a friendly dig at your best man

You know full well that your best man is going to take a few verbal pot shots at you in a few moments. Don't just meekly sit back and await his onslaught.

Get your retaliation in first. Nothing nasty or vindictive, though. All that is required is a little mild, friendly, humorous banter.

Your audience will only laugh at a parody of what it recognises as your best man's little foibles. So think about his looks, characteristics, job and hobbies. There is bound to be plenty of scope for humour here.

The guests must recognise that while all your jokes are clearly exaggerations, they are nonetheless based on fundamental truths about your best man. For instance, there is no point in laughing at his colourful use of language, unless you are sure the audience knows he spends most of his waking hours effing and blinding, and is not merely the kind who just might bleat out an apologetic 'oh, blast' – and then only if mauled by a lion.

> For a gag to work, people need to know what you're talking about.

Say he is not known for his sartorial elegance, then you might observe that:

> '(*Best man*) will be getting up to speak in a moment or two, and I can tell you he has some very unusual material, beginning with his suit.'

If he's known to be a bit of a boozer:

> 'It only takes one drink to get (*best man*) drunk . . . the fourteenth.'

If he wheels and deals in wheels:

> 'Last week, at the car lot (*best man*) pointed to an old Escort. "I can't shift this," he said, "I'll have to reduce it."

"By how much?" I asked. "Oh, by about three owners and 50,000 miles," he replied.'

If he's into photography:

'I'm not too sure what kind of photographs (best man) takes, but I can tell you he has to develop them in the dark.'

A neat little trick is to go one stage further and to damn him through faint praise. The idea here is to issue a half-hearted compliment which really does no more that highlight your poor victim's mediocrity:

'A man like (best man) only comes along once in a lifetime – I'm only sorry it had to be during my lifetime.'

'(Best man) is the most independent salesman I know. He doesn't take orders from anyone.'

'I have to tell you, that, in all the years I've known him, no one has ever questioned his intelligence. In fact, I've never heard anyone mention it.'

Finally, if you know any uncomplicated jokes or stories involving your best man, why not tell them?

➤ 3 Telling jokes and stories

There is a fundamental difference in written and spoken humour. To illustrate this let's consider how a joke can improve in the telling over the bald facts on the printed page.

Use the fact that you are on your feet to your advantage. As you tell a joke or story, wherever possible act it out. For example, suppose you want to tell the guests about a few little problems you encountered when you were the best man, not the bridegroom. You might say:

'The suit arrived with two days to spare. On trying it on I found the jacket was too tight. I rushed back to (local outfitters) to get it altered only to be told it would take at least a week. The only alternative, they said, was to hunch my shoulders a little and breathe in. I was practising this delicate technical manoeuvre in front of a mirror the next day, but as I took a step forward the seam on one trouser leg split, from top to toe. I was incensed but on ringing (outfitters) I was again told there was no time for repairs, so I should walk with my legs pressed close together to hide the split.

The day of the wedding arrived. Putting on the wretched outfit I placed my best man's speech in my trouser pocket only for it to fall straight through to the floor. I decided for safety's sake to keep my hand permanently in my pocket grasping my notes.

Walking the short distance from my house to the church – my shoulders hunched, breathing in, one leg as close to the other as possible and with my hand clasped in my pocket – I was spotted by a couple of elderly wedding guests.

"Just look at that young man over there," I heard one say, "Isn't he walking in a strange fashion."

"Oh yes," said the other, glancing across at me, ". . . . but doesn't his suit fit him well!" '

At each stage during this story – the ill-fitting jacket, the split in the trouser seam, the bottomless pocket – the humour would be greatly enhanced by a few relevant movements, gestures and expressions, culminating in your hilarious impersonation of the man from the Ministry of Silly Walks!

The precise wording and style of delivery of a joke, of course, is *yours*, not mine. But I hope this example will encourage the novice to look at his material a little more carefully to see what can be extracted over and above the obvious punchline reaction. We'll return to this topic in Chapter 5 (Paint word pictures).

➤ 4 Rehearsing a few 'ad-lib' lines

Rod Stewart sang about 'well rehearsed ad-lib lines'. You must be able to think on your feet, but it's always useful to know a few humorous lines you could use under the right circumstances.

During a wedding speech, you're most unlikely to be faced by loudmouth drunks or other nasty punters. And other interruptions, such as boisterous late comers or early leavers, are likely to be minimal. However, these things can happen, and it is best to be prepared for them. So here are some mild lines that could prove useful to counter the kind of problems or distractions you could encounter:

➤ **Your microphone starts playing up**: 'Well, Mike, that's the end of our double act; I'm going solo.'

➤ **You fluff a line**: 'Sorry, I'm breaking these teeth in for the dog.'

➤ **You forget a name**: 'I'm so sorry, there are three things I always forget: names, faces and, er, . . . I can't remember the other.'

➤ **A glass smashes**: 'I'm pleased your having such a smashing time.'

➤ **To anyone leaving**: 'S/He'll be back in a wee while.'

➤ **To anyone returning**: 'Could you hear us out there? . . . we could hear you in here.'

➤ **A catch-all when anything goes wrong**: 'I hope that camcorder is still running. That's certain to be worth £250.'

I would also counsel restraint; once you have responded to a friendly interruption or made a humorous remark about someone making a call of nature, it is best to get on with your speech and leave any further disruptions to go unnoticed.

> But don't take the rise out of anyone until you've established yourself as the likeable, loveable chap that you are.

✓ **Checklist**

Lighten your speech with touches of humour. Select a variety of relevant material that everyone present will find amusing.

Take a few carefully targeted mild pot shots at your best man ... but make it patently clear to everyone that you don't really mean a word of it.

Be more than just a talking head; act your jokes out. Be prepared to deliver one or two humorous 'ad-libs', should the circumstances demand them.

4 Finding the Ideal Beginning and Ending

A good speech has a good beginning and a good ending, both of which are kept very close together.

In this chapter:

➤ Grabbing their attention

➤ Responding to the toast of the bride and groom

➤ Ending on the right note

➤ Proposing a toast to the bridesmaids

➤ Bracketing your speech

There is no such thing as the best opening lines or the best closing lines for a bridegroom's speech, because every speech – and every speaker – is different. In this chapter you will learn a number of techniques that can be used to open and close a speech. They are all tried and tested, so you don't need to worry about choosing a dud. Study the options and decide what would work best for *your* speech – and for *you*.

There are dozens of ways to put over a captivating opening or to deliver a compelling close. It's just a matter of finding the pattern of words that suits your style and has exactly the effect you are after. Work on your lines until you've got them spot on. Then **memorise** them or write them out on a card to use as a prompt. You must know *precisely* how you are going to open and close your speech. There is absolutely no room for any ad-libbing here.

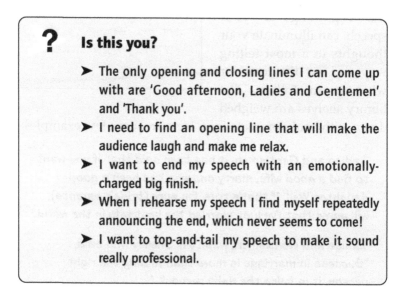

? **Is this you?**

- ➤ The only opening and closing lines I can come up with are 'Good afternoon, Ladies and Gentlemen' and 'Thank you'.
- ➤ I need to find an opening line that will make the audience laugh and make me relax.
- ➤ I want to end my speech with an emotionally-charged big finish.
- ➤ When I rehearse my speech I find myself repeatedly announcing the end, which never seems to come!
- ➤ I want to top-and-tail my speech to make it sound really professional.

➤ **1 Grabbing their attention**

It is **essential to start well**. Allow yourself plenty of time to find an effective opening.

It is vital to have an opening line that really grabs your audience's attention. Entertainers call this having a hook. For the bridegroom, undoubtedly the most useful varieties are:

➤ the quotation hook

➤ the anniversary hook

➤ the humour hook

The quotation hook

The right quotation, told at the beginning of your speech, can illuminate your thoughts in a most telling way and set the tone for what is to follow. The library shelves are weighed down with books of quotations. Here are just a few examples:

> Successful speakers often ponder, consciously and unconsciously, for days over their opening words. They know that the first three sentences of their speech set the course for success or failure: a good start points towards plain sailing, a bad one makes you sail against the wind.

'Ladies and Gentlemen, it has been said that if you want to find a good wife, marry one who has been a good daughter. Well, if that's true, I'm sure (*bride's parents*) will agree that I've just married the best wife in the world.'

'Ladies and Gentlemen, wasn't it Shelley who said, "Success in marriage is more than *finding* the right person, it is *being* the right person". '

'Ladies and Gentlemen . . . I've heard it said that getting married is like getting a dog. It teaches you to be less self-centred; to expect sudden, surprising outbursts of affection; and not to be upset by a few scratches on your car . . .'

The anniversary hook

There's nothing like telling people what a special day it is today. You're telling them that 'Today's the Day!' As always, use your own words, but this is the sort of thing you should say:

'Ladies and Gentlemen, this is a historic day! This day, the 30th of September will always be remembered because of three very famous events. Tony Blackburn played the first-ever record on Radio One – the Move's *Flowers in the Rain* – back in 1967; tennis ace Martina Hingis was born in 1980; and on this day in 201X, I married (*bride*)!'

'Ladies and Gentlemen, this is a day heavy with significance! This very day, the 1st of June, will always be associated with three truly historic events. Screen legend Marilyn Monroe was born in 1926 . . . The Beatles released the classic *Sergeant Pepper's Lonely Hearts Club Band* in 1967 . . . and on this day in 201X, you heard the finest damn wedding speech of your entire lifetime! Now . . . who's going to make it?'

You can find plenty of birthdays and anniversaries listed in specialist anniversary books. You'll also find them in most daily and Sunday newspapers.

The humour hook

Opening with a short and relevant gag will help you to relax and get the audience laughing. Here are just a few examples of jokey openings that you could use or adapt to hook your guests:

'Good Ladies, afternoon and Gentlemen . . . I *knew* I should have rehearsed this speech.'

'Ladies and Gentlemen, this afternoon I'm speaking free of charge, and I'm sure you'll soon agree I'm worth every penny of it.'

'Ladies and Gentlemen, thank you – please keep applauding.
I've got a very weak finish . . . or so (wife) tells me.'

Consider other ideas too. There are so many new, exciting and
unconventional openings.
Look for a method that **fits
your personality**. Then **test
your opening**. Have you
used just the right words, in
the right order, with the
right timing?

> If you can leave your
> opening lines out altogether
> and it's not a loss, look for
> some better ones.

Then **memorise** and **practise** them. Rehearse, rehearse and
rehearse. If your first sentence does not make an impact, you
will lose your chance for immediate success. You only have
one chance to make a good first impression.

➤ 2 Responding to the toast to the bride and groom

Remember that tradition and good manners demand that you
respond to the bride's father's toast to you and your new wife.
Unless she's going to speak
for herself, make it clear
that you are speaking on
behalf of both of you.

> All that is required of you is
> a brief acknowledgement
> of the toast immediately
> before or soon after you
> hook your audience. Once
> that's out of the way you
> can forget it and get on
> with your speech.

'First of all, my wife and I
. . . oh, how I've waited to
say those four little
words . . . my wife and I

wish to thank (*bride's father*), for those warm-hearted words. I do not deserve the good things you said of me . . . but I shall try to deserve them, and be worthy of my wife.'

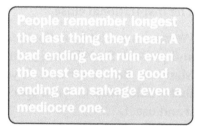

Your opening sentence is the second most important sentence of your speech. Yes, you've guessed it: the most important sentence is your last.

➤ 3 Ending on the right note

Try to end with a flourish. Your concluding remarks should be to a speaker what a high note is to a singer: the candescence that triggers spontaneous cheers and applause. If you can find the ideal ending you will inject that ultimate bit of magic.

People remember longest the last thing they hear. A bad ending can ruin even the best speech; a good ending can salvage even a mediocre one.

The ending, like the opening, is too important to be left to the mercy of chance or the whim of the moment. It does not have to be long and complicated – indeed, it should not be – but it does have to be worked out in advance and well rehearsed.

There are many ways to wind up a speech. However, remember that **every speech needs its own ending**, tailored to its tone, content and participants. The following list therefore is intended as no more than a broad spectrum of possibilities:

➤ the sentimental close

➤ the inspirational close

➤ the shock close

➤ the wit and wisdom close

➤ the unexpected toast close

The sentimental close

A wedding is an emotional occasion and your speech should reflect this. If you mean something deeply, then say it out loud from the heart with courage, confidence and conviction: 'Maggie, I love you!'

The inspirational close

We can learn a lot from the great inspirational speakers of past and present: Sir Winston Churchill, John F. Kennedy, Nelson Mandela, Barack Obama. If you find an ideal uplifting line that would wrap up your speech perfectly, then grab it, adapt it and use it.

Martin Luther King concluded his famous 'I have a dream' speech with these words: 'Free at last! Free at last! Thank God Almighty, free at last!' This powerful three-phrase close could be adapted to: 'Together at last! Together at last! Thank God, we're together at last!'

The shock close

The idea here is to make an apparently outrageous or shocking statement. Then, after a brief pause, to clarify yourself. Your audience's relief will be audible:

'Finally, I have a confession to make. When I took my vows in church today, I lied. I did *not* marry for better or worse . . . I married for good!'

The wit and wisdom close

Some speakers end with a good joke while others prefer to impart a pearl of wisdom. Why not do both? Why not use humour to illustrate a universal truth?

A shrewdly chosen line or verse which combines truth with fun is a far more popular finale than a glum old proverb.

These three 'let-me-leave-you-with-this-thought' gems come from Bob Monkhouse, Groucho Marx and Pam Eyres:

'My dad taught me that marriage is an investment that pays dividends if you pay interest . . . and that's more than mere speculation. Believe me, I'm going to pay a great deal of interest!'

'Even when a marriage is made in heaven, the maintenance work has to be done on earth . . . and, let me tell you, I'm never going to stop working at it!'

'Love is like a curry and I'll explain to you, that love comes in three temperatures: medium, hot and vindaloo. . . . ours is *extra hot* vindaloo.'

The unexpected toast close

You are not *expected* to propose a toast to your wife, but if you do, immediately before the traditional toast to the brides-maids, the effect will be impressive:

'Here's to my mother-in-law's daughter,
Here's to my father's son;
And here's to the vows
we've just taken,
And to the life we've just
begun!'

'A toast to my wife: Never
above you. Never below
you. Always beside you.'

'To my wife:
May we always share love
and laughter!'

> The conclusion then, is the highlight of your speech, your final burst. Plan it well and practise it. The last sentence must come out perfectly. It will linger in the mind a little more than everything that went before.

➤ 4 Proposing a toast to the bridesmaids

Don't forget to propose that toast to the bridesmaids. All you need to do is to add a few thankful and congratulatory words after your big finish, for example:

> Whichever variety of close you choose, don't forget to add a toast!

'Finally, what can I say about the bridesmaids, the charming young ladies who did such a great job in helping (*wife*) up the aisle . . . although I hope she came to the church of her own free will! They have been wonderful and added so much to the occasion, so please join me in drinking a toast to the bridesmaids. Ladies and Gentlemen, the bridesmaids!'

➤5 Bracketing your speech

This is a device usually associated with seasoned pros. It is designed not only to grab an audience's attention at the *start* of a speech, but also – and at the same time – to set up a situation that can be exploited at the *end*. The idea is to present your speech as a **satisfying whole**, not just as a series of stories, jokes and reminiscences, however well they may have been crafted and structured.

> Bracketing is a wonderful way of linking an attention-grabbing opening with a humorous, romantic or emotionally-charged big finish.

The two brackets consist of a **set-up** at the opening of the speech and a **pay-off** at the end. The words you will end with include those planted clearly at the start, like this:

Set-up: 'Ladies and Gentlemen, they say love is blind. Well I certainly can't see far ahead . . . not without my glasses . . . and I readily admit that in the past at times I've been a bit shortsighted . . . and sometimes even made a bit of a spectacle out of myself . . . But today, with or without my glasses, I can see my future mapped out very clearly . . .'

Pay-off: 'You know, today, for the first time in my life, I don't need to wear glasses to see what a bright and wonderful future lies ahead of me . . . And right now I really couldn't give a damn that I'm a

bit shortsighted. Why should I? . . . Love is blind.
And, in any case, all I need to see is (bride) . . .'

Notice how the repetition of the words 'glasses', 'shortsighted'
and 'love is blind' helps the open-and-closed nature of the
brackets and provides a pleasing and memorable symmetry.

✓ **Checklist**

Think of your speech as a gourmet meal. Your opening
lines should serve up a tasty little starter that really
whets the audience's appetite for the main course.
Your closing words should provide a delectable and
memorable desert with a delicious aftertaste.

Don't forget to respond to the bride's father's toast ...

And don't forget to propose a toast to the bridesmaids!

You must end on a high note: humorous, romantic,
inspiring. Plan it well and practise it. The final sentence must come out perfectly. It is the last
impression you leave with your audience.

Your speech can be made truly memorable by plant-
ing a bracket at the beginning and matching one at
the end.

5 Putting It All Together

To create a memorable wedding speech requires excitement, empathy, warmth, enthusiasm and flair. Flair is the sizzle in the sausage.

In this chapter:

➤ Preparing your script
➤ Using words to be said, not read
➤ Adding a sparkle to your speech
➤ Remembering rhythm
➤ Keeping it flowing

Having something worthwhile to say is *never* enough. You need to know how to use words and images to reach your audience's minds and hearts. Your speech **needs a touch of flair**. Flair is partly intuition – which comes from experience, imagination and a willingness to think – and a careful study of this chapter!

Every communication is an opportunity to throw a bridge across a void. If you can do this, your speech will have more effect than you could ever have believed possible. When we face an important interview, we prepare ourselves to make the best possible impression. We look good. So, if we are about to meet an audience, we should polish our words as well as our shoes. We should sound good.

Today people's expectations are high and their attention spans are low. Merely to gain and hold an audience's attention requires flair. If you want to keep them interested, your speech must sparkle. So let's get polishing.

? Is this you?

➤ I don't know what sort of script to prepare – if any.

➤ The last time I made a speech I think I must have sounded as if I was reading the news. I was too matter of fact.

➤ I want my speech to be more than just an unconnected series of thoughts and reminiscences.

➤ Of course I want what I say to convey my emotions and be entertaining, but I also want what I say to sound good.

➤ I want to make a speech I can be truly proud of!

➤1 Preparing your script

The best talkers are those who are the most natural. They are easy, fluent, friendly and amusing. No script for them. How could there be? They are talking only to us and basing what they say on our reactions as they go along. For most of us, however, that sort of performance is an aspiration rather than a description. Our tongues are not so honeyed and our words are less winged. We need a script.

But what sort of script? Cards? Notes? Speech written out in full? It's up to you. There is no right way of doing it. Here is a simple method favoured by many speakers:

➤ Write the speech out **in full**.

➤ **Memorise** the opening and closing lines and **familiarise** yourself with the remainder of the speech.

➤ **Summarise** the speech on one card or one sheet of paper using **key words** to remind you of your **sequence** of anecdotes, quotations, jokes and so on.

The main advantage of this method is that the speaker will not only be sure to cover everything he wants to, but will also come across as a natural and spontaneous speaker who is not merely reciting a prepared speech.

➤2 Using words to be said, not read

Most people can write something to be *read*, few can write something to be *said*. Indeed, most people are unaware that there is even a difference.

We are used to writing things to be read: by our lecturers, our friends, our relatives, our bosses, our work colleagues. Such everyday written communication is known as **text**. What we are not used to doing is speaking our written words out loud. Writing intended to be spoken and heard is known as **script**.

Every effective speaker *must* recognise that there are very important differences between text and script, namely:

Text	Script
➤ is a journey at the reader's pace	➤ is a journey at the speaker's pace
➤ can be re-read, if necessary	➤ is heard once, and only once
➤ can be read in any order	➤ is heard in the order it is spoken

Therefore, you must prepare a speech for an audience which *cannot* listen at its own pace; which *cannot* ask you to repeat parts it did not hear or understand and which *cannot* choose the order in which to consider your words.

> We seem subconsciously to understand the best words and phrases and the best order of words and phrases when we speak, but we seem to lose the knack when we write script.

Consider how the same sentiment might be conveyed by a writer, first using text and then script:

Text:

The meaning of marriage is not to be found in church services, or in romantic novels or films. We have no right to expect a happy ending. The meaning of marriage is to be found in all the effort that is required to make a marriage succeed. You need to get to know your partner, and thereby to get to know yourself.

Script:

'The meaning of marriage isn't to be found in wedding bells ... it isn't the stuff of Mills and Boon romances ... there is no happy ever after. No, the meaning of marriage is in the trying and it's about learning about someone else ... and through that learning about yourself.'

The lesson is clear: **speak your words aloud before you commit them to paper**. You will find that each element, each phrase, each sentence, will be built from what has gone before. Instinctively, you will take your listeners from the **known** to the **unknown**; from the **general** to the **particular**; from the **present** to the **future**.

➤ **3** Adding a sparkle to your speech

➤ **Paint word pictures**: watching a story unfold before your eyes is dramatic and memorable. The characters move. The scenes are in colour. The whole thing has life. Merely listening to a wordy description, however enthusiastically delivered, is a yawn.

Today most people are used to *watching* TV, not *listening* to radio. You need give your jokes and stories a graphic quality. People will appreciate this because it is what they are used to. The way to do this is not to tell jokes and stories, but to paint word pictures that allow your audience's own imagination to take over. Don't just tell a gag, paint it:

> 'Let me tell you something about my best man. Soon after we met, Dave invited me to his eighteenth birthday party and he gave me details of his address and how to get there. He said, "A number 8 bus will bring you right to my door – 69 Della Street. Walk up to the front door and press the doorbell with your elbow." "Why my elbow?" I asked. "Because you'll have the wine in one hand and my prezzie in the other, won't you?" '

Use words and images creatively and imaginatively and your speech will come to life. Things happen in the minds and hearts of your audience. If you look into their eyes, you can see it happen. It's a great experience.

Give your audience the right detail and they can see your word picture. And one picture is worth a thousand words.

➤ **Use figurative language**: try to make your speech colourful and original. Similes and metaphors are particularly useful devices. A **simile** is a figure of speech, usually introduced by *like* or *as*, that **compares** one thing to another:

> 'Our love germinated *like* a seed in the dark.'

> 'Our love is *as* eternal *as* the sea and the wind.'

Because a simile's function is comparison, it is not as evocative as a metaphor. A **metaphor** does not so much compare as

transform one thing to another. It is more subtle and revealing, stimulating imagery beyond the original transformation:

> 'With the two of us it is just as it is with the honeysuckle that attaches itself to the hazel tree: when it has wound and attached itself around the trunk, the two can survive together; but if someone tries to separate them, the hazel dies quickly and the honeysuckle with it. Sweet love, so it is with us: you cannot live without me, nor I without you.'

Those words were spoken by Marie de France over 800 years ago – and they work just as well today.

Another useful figure of speech is **hyperbole**, or deliberately overstating your argument. In a wedding speech you can get away with saying things that most people would find embarrassing and even crass in everyday conversation:

> 'You are the best parents in the world.'

Not only can you get away with it – such bizarre overstatement can be highly effective, bringing a lump to the throat and a tear to the eye:

> 'I'll love you till the ocean is folded and hung up to dry, and the seven stars go squawking like geese about the sky.'

➤ **Engage all the senses**: sensory details bring breadth and depth to your descriptions. We can learn a lot from writers of popular fiction. Take a look at this extract from *The Fallen Curtain* by Ruth Rendell:

> Tea was lovely at gran's. Fish and chips that she didn't fetch from the shop but cooked herself, cream meringues and chocolate éclairs, tinned peaches with evaporated milk, the lot washed down with fizzy lemonade.

How much more effective this is than simply saying, 'Gran doted on me and spoilt me something rotten at tea-time'.

Here Stephen King uses sensory details to bring a character to life in *Carrie*:

> Norma led them around the dance floor to their table. She exuded odours of Avon soap, Woolworth's perfume and Juicy Fruit gum.

And how about this from Katherine Mansfield:

> Alexander and his friend in a train. Spring . . . wet lilac . . . spouting rain.

So few words yet the wetness is palpable.

➤ **Make good use of symbolism**: symbolism – employing a visual metaphor to underline a theme – is a natural aspect of communication. Children at play instinctively use symbols, making items 'stand for' aspects of their imaginary games. Advertisers strive to connect their products with abstract notions like success, nostalgia, or domestic bliss – thus a floor cleaner symbolically represents freedom (through liberation from household chores), while a téte-à-téte coffee symbolises passionate liaison.

Bah, humbug? Maybe, but it works. You'll find symbols in most adverts. And the colour red crops up a lot: a red sunset to advertise a liquor, a bowl of red roses behind a bottle of scent, and of course all those obligatory red sports cars. Red is warm. It is vibrant, a symbol of passion, excitement and romance. When

> Symbolism, like perfect pastry, requires a light hand. The aim is to allow implication to resonate through significant detail, not to overload description with obscure riddles or hackneyed images.

you want to suggest these things, use a strong symbol that will arouse the audience's feelings and describe a variety of hot colours, especially red:

> 'I took a walk in the park this morning. Every bush, every tree trembled with the fluttering of butterflies – beautiful red butterflies. It was magnificent. Yesterday there were no butterflies in my garden. Today there are thousands. Tomorrow there will be millions.'

➤ 4 Remembering rhythm

A good speech, should attract and hold listeners as a magnet attracts and holds iron filings. Here are a few more techniques that will grab your audience and add an enchanting, tuneful quality to your speech:

➤ **The rule of three**: three is a magical number. People love to hear speakers talk to the beat of three. The effect of three words, three phrases or three sentences is powerful and memorable:

'My mother gave me hope . . . she gave me courage . . . but most of all, she gave me love.'

'Someone said that a true friend is a person who understands your past, believes in your future, and accepts you today just the way you are. If that's true, (*best man*) is the best friend I have ever had.'

'(*Bride*), from this day forth real joy will fill your days . . . warm your nights . . . and overflow your heart forever.'

➤ **Parallel sentences**: sentences that are parallel add a rhythmic beauty that help an audience anticipate and follow your thoughts:

'Marriage is a celebration of love. Marriage is a celebration of life. Marriage is a celebration of joy.'

➤ **Alliteration**: the repetition of sounds and syllables, usually at the beginning of words, can help create just the right mood. Your speech will become special and spellbinding:

'You are the most wonderful woman in the world . . . and I worship you!'

➤ **Repetition**: if there is anything almost guaranteed to make an audience break out in spontaneous applause it is a repetition of strong, emotive words:

'I will love you for ever . . . and ever . . . and ever!'

However, use the wrong words and it will fall flat. How does this sound?

'I will think the world of
you indefinitely . . .
indefinitely . . .
indefinitely!'

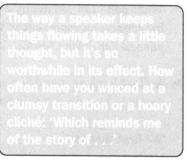

Using words colourfully and
creatively will bring your
speech to life like a shot of
whisky in a cup of coffee.

It doesn't work, does it?

➤ **5** Keeping it flowing

Have you noticed how entertainers, politicians and TV pre-
senters move **easily** and
unobtrusively from one
topic to another? Like them,
you can make your speech
flow **smoothly** and **gracefully** from beginning to end
by making use of a few of
these simple devices:

The way a speaker keeps
things flowing takes a little
thought, but it's so
worthwhile in its effect. How
often have you winced at a
clumsy transition or a hoary
cliché: 'Which reminds me
of the story of . . .'

➤ **A bridge** is a word that
alerts an audience that
you are changing direction or moving to a new thought:

'So that's how I met (bride). But romance didn't blossom
right away . . .'

➤ **A trigger** is a repetition of the same word or phrase to link
one topic with another:

'That was what (bride) was like at school. Now I'll tell you
what she was like at college . . .'

➤ **A rhetorical question** is a question which you ask – and answer:

'How do you think my dashing best man spent yesterday evening? . . .'

Some members of the audience may know both you and the bride very well, while others may only know one of you. Asking a rhetorical question is also an excellent way of telling people something while not insulting the intelligence of those already in the know:

'What can I tell you about a girl who won the school prize for geography, represented the county at netball and passed her driving test . . . at the sixth attempt?'

➤ **A flashback** is a sudden shift to the past to break what seems to be a predictable narrative:

'We first met in . . .'
'We both worked for . . .'
'We started going out together when . . .' (yawn, yawn!)

It would have been far more interesting to have provided an unexpected flashback link, such as:

'Today she's the confident, woman-about-town you see before you. But five years ago she wasn't like that . . .'

➤ **A list** is a very simple way of combining apparently unre-lated incidents:

'I remember three occasions when I got into trouble with my parents . . .'

But don't rely too heavily on lists because a catalogue of events soon becomes extremely tedious to listen to.

➤ **A pause** is a non-verbal way of showing your audience that you have finished one section of your speech and are about to move on to another.

➤ **A physical movement** is another non-verbal signal that you are moving on to something new. If you turn to the bride, your audience know that you are going to talk to her, or about her.

➤ **A quotation, joke or story** can also serve as an excellent link. Here a neat little one-liner is used to change the topic from *how well-suited you are* to *you*:

'. . . so this really is a love match, pure and simple; (*bride's*) pure and I'm . . . a very nice man . . .'

✓ **Checklist**

Rehearse using a variety of types of script — cards, notes, speech written out in full — before deciding which one suits you best.

Think like a listener and write like a talker. Say your words aloud before you commit them to paper. Use **effective** language, not necessarily correct language.

Use words and images creatively and imaginatively so they reach your audience's minds and touch their hearts.

It is important that what you say **sounds** good. Your speech should have its own rhythm. Give it light and shade, valleys and peaks. Just as the varied rhythm and intensity of a fireworks display adds anticipation and excitement, so a landscape of valleys and peaks will keep an audience interested and involved. People need valleys before they can see peaks.

Make sure your speech flows **smoothly** and **gracefully** from beginning to end.

6 Getting the Delivery Right

Once you accept that you can approach your wedding speech in exactly the same way as you approach informal communication, your apprehension will dwindle and your confidence will soar.

In this chapter:

➤ Being conversational
➤ Projecting your personality
➤ Being heard

These goals may sound glaringly obvious, yet few public speakers even consider them.

This chapter will *not* put you in a straitjacket of artificial presentation techniques. You will not be told how to stand, how to gesticulate, how to look at people, how to talk. In everyday life you have no trouble with any of these skills, and the **combinations in which you use them make up your personality**.

If you abandon everything that is natural to you and substitute 'acquired' mannerisms, is it really surprising that you will come over as unnatural, awkward and insincere?

Whatever individual characteristics you have that are special to you should be nurtured and cultivated and worked on, for it is these personal and unique quirks of appearance, personality and expression that will mark you out as a speaker with something different to offer. And that is never a bad thing.

? Is this you?

➤ Immediately before I start speaking in public I feel very wound up and wish I wasn't there.

➤ The last time I made a speech it felt like I was standing aside from myself, listening to a voice that didn't belong to me. It was very strange.

➤ As I stand up in front of an audience a kind of lead veil comes over me and all I can see is a close-up of myself. I hear my voice in a very loud way and every word I utter sounds awful.

➤ I have a very dull voice.

➤ When I speak in public, my voice dries up and it destroys all the natural flow, all the rhythms and any kind of creative spark or anecdote that might come in is destroyed. Terrible.

➤ **1** Being conversational

When you are sitting leisurely, with family, friends or colleagues, your conversation will be naturally relaxed and chatty, because that is the language of **easy communication**. When you make a speech, the words and phrases you use should be more **considered, imaginative, creative** and **rhythmical** than your everyday language, yet the way you say them, the way you deliver your speech should remain unaffectedly relaxed and chatty.

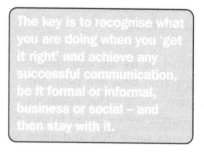

Talk to your audience just as you would to John and Jane Smith. What is the audience, after all, but a collection of John and Jane Smiths?

If you are different when you make a speech in public, you may be perceived as phoney, boring, or lacking in personality. As a result, people will not take to you and they certainly will not be convinced by, or remember, much of what you have to say.

The key is to recognise what you are doing when you 'get it right' and achieve any successful communication, be it formal or informal, business or social – and then stay with it.

Certainly you may need to speak a little louder or make other concessions to accommodate the needs of your audience, but, in essence, nothing in your delivery style should change. **You should be yourself made large.**

You need to recognise, and then capture this normal style of communication and make it work for you, naturally, **in any given situation**, regardless of the stress level. When you walk into your office or a restaurant or a greengrocer's shop, you don't hover outside anxiously rehearsing how you will deliver your lines.

We all communicate each day without fear of failure. If you can understand how normal, relaxed, **informal** spoken communication works, you will be able to understand what you must do, and keep on doing during **formal** spoken communication.

Your conversational abilities are far more practised than your literary abilities. Casual conversation is not constructed in a literary way. You do not always finish your sentences. You repeat yourself. You use ungrammatical constructions – but you are obeying a different set of rules.

During everyday casual conversation you are obeying the rules of effective spoken communication which have been learnt, instinctively, down the ages. Don't abandon these rules when you speak in public.

Most of us are astonished the first time we hear our own voice. The resonant sounds we've heard in our heads seem thin and alien issuing from an audio or video player. It doesn't matter. Think about some of our top entertainers and most effective communicators: Chris Evans, Graham Norton, Jeremy Clarkson. None of these gifted talkers would win prizes at RADA. There is nothing of the mighty orator about any of them. All these famous and successful individuals stopped worrying about their voices long ago, if they ever did. They are each concerned with **putting across their ideas**. They speak to us with clarity, cheerfulness, and charm – and sometimes conviction.

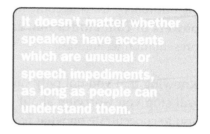

It doesn't matter whether speakers have accents which are unusual or speech impediments, as long as people can understand them.

➤ 2 Projecting your personality

Your personality is your greatest asset. It is personal chemistry that makes people want to be friends with other people. Very few of us, given the choice, will choose to associate with someone we don't like or trust.

Think carefully about **how you come across** when you communicate effortlessly under everyday circumstances. Probably you will not have considered this before. It is an extremely useful exercise because it makes you appreciate what you must also do during your speeches.

When a person talks informally, they probably sit or stand in a relaxed manner, breathing naturally, maintaining an appropriate level of eye contact, gesturing every now and then to reinforce their words, and smiling at intervals to establish and maintain rapport. Yet the moment this same person stands up to address

The moment you are told to do something in a certain way you become conscious of what you should be doing naturally.

an audience, they become nervous, distrust their **innate powers of communication**, and rely on a range of artificial presentation techniques.

Knowing that you not only can, but also should 'be yourself' will stop you worrying about your 'performance', and allow you to concentrate on what really matters: being sincere, emotional and witty.

Each speaker is unique; each speaker has a **unique style**. What might be most effective for one person would be a disaster for another. Did Elvis, Sinatra and Johnny Rotten all sound the same singing *My Way*? Of course not. The artist makes the crucial difference. So, too, does the speaker.

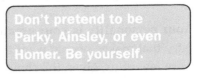

Don't pretend to be Parky, Ainsley, or even Homer. Be yourself.

We all have *some* abilities and talents. Don't hide your light under a bushel. Any regional accents or dialects which you can do well (and only if you *can* do them well) should be incorporated into your stories. A punchline is doubled in effect in the appropriate Cockney or Brummie accent, especially after a 'straight' and serious build up.

Have you any funny faces, impersonations or mannerisms of speech which infallibly convulse friends and relatives at parties? These eccentricities, suitably broadened out, might work just as well at the reception.

➤ **3** Being heard

If there is public address equipment available, find out how it works, try to get some practice and then use it.

If there is no sound-enhancing equipment, **speak as clearly and as loudly as is necessary to be heard**. If the only other person in the room was at the back, you would talk to him or her naturally,

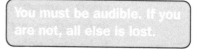

You must be audible. If you are not, all else is lost.

at the right level, without shouting or straining, by:

➤ keeping your head up

➤ opening your mouth wider than during normal speech

➤ using clearer consonants

➤ slowing down.

If you remember that you must be heard by the person who is farthest from you, during your speech, however many other people may be in the room, you will make those same four natural adjustments to your delivery.

✓ **Checklist**

Don't abandon the rules of effective spoken communication when you make your wedding speech. Get back to basics, *get conversational*.

A great deal of so-called expert advice can remove the imperfections that make us distinctive and create unremarkable clones. Stop worryng about your 'performance'. Rehearse not to be perfect but to be *comfortable*. Concentrate on what really matters: being sincere, emotional and witty.

Become *yourself made large* and make sure everyone present can *hear* you.

7 Stories, Jokes and One-liners for Your Speech

The main purposes of a bridegroom's speech are to thank everyone who has helped organise the wedding and to show that you understand the importance and significance of the occasion. The best way to do this, without sounding a complete wally in front of your mates, is to be both emotional and humorous. Like the man who slapped a cheerful old lady conducting a seance, your aim is to strike a happy medium.

This chapter provides a miscellany of jokes and humorous stories which can be told as they appear, or can be adapted and personalised to suit the occasion. I will provide you with plenty of material ranging from mild one-liners – to quite saucy stories which sensitive souls may find rather raw.

Only you know how broadminded your wife and the guests are likely to be, so choose your stories and jokes with care. Aim to be amusing, but not *too* risqué. Tell a couple of relevant and entertaining stories, and get a few mild pre-emptive strikes in against your best man before he begins his inevitable character assassination of you.

When it comes to questions of taste and taboos, things continually change. You have to keep up with the times. The important thing to remember is that a wedding is a **family** occasion. So relax and have a good laugh ... but don't go over the top!

Another thing to bear in mind is that many of the best stories, jokes and one-liners about love and marriage are quite cynical ... and there is absolutely no place for anything negative or sneering in a wedding speech. A simple way to get round this apparent dilemma is to make it abundantly clear that any cynical views expressed in your jokes most certainly do *not* apply to you or your new bride, perhaps by *reversing* the gag, like this:

> 'My wife recently joined the string section of the town orchestra. She practises day and night. She's always harping on about something or other ... Well angels do, don't they?'

Finally, always apply the Bob Monkhouse Test to potential material (see page 22). Ask yourself:

1. Do *you* think it is funny?

2. Can you say it confidently and with comfort?

3. Is there any danger of offending anyone?

4. Will they understand and appreciate it?

If a story, joke or one-liner passes this test with flying colours, it could well merit a place within your speech. Now for those jokes:

Ladies and Gentlemen, as Henry VIII said to each of his wives in turn, 'I shall not keep you long.'

A couple go out on a blind date and the boy asks the girl what she wants to do. She says, 'I want to be weighed.' He thinks this odd, but to keep her contented, he takes her to a weighing machine. 'Now what do you want to do?' he asks. And she says, 'I want to be weighed.' So off they go to find another weighing machine. He once again asks, 'And now what do you what to do?' and he gets the same reply. Thinking the girl to be totally deranged, he rapidly makes his excuses, takes her back to her student house, and leaves her with no more than a handshake. Her room-mate, Laura, asks her what the date was like, 'How did it go?' And the girl replies, 'Oh Waura, it was wousy!'

Martin has an open mind about things. You can feel the wind from here.

My sister appreciates the simple things in life. She's going out with Simon.

A newlywed bride was asked what she thought of married life compared to being single. 'Oh, there's not much difference,' she replied. 'I used to stay up half the night waiting for Jim to go, and now I stay up half the night waiting for him to come home.'

I think the world of Keith. Mind you, look at the state the world's in.

I think Jerry's suit looks terrific. I know he won't mind if I let you into a little secret – he always wears it when he goes to our monthly football social evenings. As he left the church today, his little boy grabbed him by the arm and asked him why he was wearing it when he knew it always gave him such a headache the next morning.

The last time I made a speech a man fell asleep. So I asked a waiter to wake him, and do you know what the cheeky so-and-so replied? He said, 'You wake him. You were the one who sent him to sleep.'

When Stan dies, his sad demise won't be listed in the Obituaries Column, it will be recorded under 'Neighbourhood Improvements'.

A lad goes into his girlfriend's house for the first time and she shows him into the living room. She excuses herself and goes into the kitchen to pour a couple of drinks. As the boy stands there alone, he sees an unusual looking pot on the mantelpiece. He walks over and goes to pick it up. At that moment, the girl returns to the room. He asks, 'What's this?' She replies, 'Oh, it's my father's ashes.' He says, 'I'm so very sorry ... I didn't know.' And the girl says, 'He's too lazy to go to the kitchen to get an ashtray.'

Thank you for all your wonderful gifts. I can't tell you how much they mean to us – but I should have a better idea after the honeymoon, once I've spoken to the guy in the pawn shop.

I thought about including a couple of double-entendres – you know, gags with double meanings. But then I thought – no I won't, because Ryan wouldn't get either of them.

Paul told me he bought his suit for a ridiculous figure ...
Looking at him today, I'm afraid I must agree.

After yet another argument, the newlywed bride says,
'One more word from you and I'm going home to Mother.'
Her husband replies, 'Taxi!'

Being a romantic sort of girl, Edwina insisted on getting
married in her grandmother's dress today. She looks
absolutely fabulous – but her poor old granny is freezing
to death.

Beth's cooking melts in your mouth. I wish she'd defrost
it first.

About a year ago, I told June that I dreamt I was married
to the sexiest, most intelligent woman in the world. And
she replied, 'Were we happy?'

A man tells his mate that he has had a tattoo of a £50
note put on his plonker. 'Whatever for?' asks the friend.
The man replies, 'For three reasons. First, I like playing
with my money. Second, I like to watch my money grow.
And third, and most importantly, the next time my wife
wants to blow £50, she can stay at home and do it.'

When I first met Louise, she told me I only had two faults
– everything I said and everything I did.

This is the first time I have spoken at a wedding, except
during other people's speeches.

A golfer slices his ball into the woods and goes in to find it. There he meets a girl from the adjoining fairway, who is looking for her ball. They start to chat and get on really well. He tells her of his recent good fortune when he became a Lottery millionaire. After a while longer, she says to him, 'You know, you look like my third husband ... you really could be him.' 'Really?' he responds, 'How many times have you been married?' The girl answers, 'Twice.'

Julie broke off her engagement to Will. I asked her what happened, and she said, 'I thought it was love at first sight, and it was ... but it was the second and third times I looked that changed my mind.'

I want to refute the vicious rumour that's been going round here today that we *had* to get married. That's a wicked lie. We could have waited another fortnight.

Charlie is rather fond of Lisa. He gave her a box of chocolates on her birthday, saying, 'Here you are, sweets for the sweet.' 'Oh, thanks,' Lisa replied, 'Have some nuts.'

'If you'll make the toast and pour the orange juice, breakfast will be ready,' announced the newlywed bride. 'Good. What's for breakfast?' asked her husband. His wife replied, 'Toast and orange juice.'

This marriage will last a lifetime. And, as you know, that's unusual these days. I know a couple who broke up before their wedding pictures were developed ... and they were using a Polaroid camera.

Like the two acrobats who got married, we're both head over heels in love!

The last time I made a speech, someone at the back shouted, 'I can't hear you!' And a man sitting next to me yelled back, 'I'll change places with you!'

James told me that when he gets married, he's is going to abandon his rural life and go to live in the city. I asked him why and he said, 'I'll be much safer in a city, because they say the country may be going to war.'

I hear Angela doesn't care for a man's company. Not unless he owns it.

A newlywed wife says to her husband, 'Darling, the woman next door has got a coat exactly like mine.' The husband responds, 'I suppose that's a hint you want a new coat?' And the wife replies, 'Well, it would be a lot cheaper than moving to a new house.'

We've found a great way to settle our arguments; she admits she's wrong and I admit I'm right.

If your wife is shouting at the front door, and your dog is barking at the back door, who do you let in first? The dog, of course. At least he'll shut up when you let him in.

A newlywed husband asked his wife whether she had sewn a button on his coat. 'No, darling,' she replied, 'I couldn't find a button. But it's alright. I sewed up the buttonhole.'

When a young couple return from their honeymoon, the wife runs to the phone to call her mother, who asks, 'How was the honeymoon, dear?' 'Mummy,' she replies, 'it was so wonderful and romantic ... but as soon as we returned home, he started using the most disgusting language ... I mean, all those nasty 4-letter words.' 'Oh, how awful!' her mother exclaims, 'What words did he use?' The wife replies, 'Horrible words like DUST, IRON, WASH, COOK ... !'

Steve told me that a gorgeous girl at the bar was getting on his nerves. 'But she's not even looking at you,' I said. He replied, 'That's what's getting on my nerves.'

Pat's friends go clubbing on Saturdays, sowing their wild oats. On Sunday mornings you'll find them praying for a crop failure.

My wife said she didn't believe in love at first sight. It took her few dates to find the size of my assets.

Jim and Alice had just returned from their honeymoon and were having their first argument. No matter what Jim tried to do or say, Alice refused to compromise or even listen. Jim started to become extremely exasperated, and he said, 'When we got married, you promised to love, honour and obey.' Alice replied, 'I know. I didn't want to start an argument in front of all those people in the church.'

Sue broke off her engagement to Adam. I asked her what had happened, and she said, 'My feelings towards him aren't the same any more.' 'Are you giving the ring back?' I asked. Sue replied, 'No, my feelings for the ring haven't changed.'

Martin, the avant-garde painter, got married. A few weeks later, someone asked his wife, 'Louise, how's married life?' 'It's great,' she answered. 'My husband paints and I cook. Then we try to guess what he's painted and what I've cooked.'

A newlywed bride has a bad hair day. So she treats her scalp with olive oil, before washing it. Worried that the oil would leave an odour, she proceeds to rinse it several times. That night, when they are in bed, she leans over her husband and asks, 'Do I smell like olive oil?' He takes a quick sniff, and says, 'No, dear. Do I smell like Popeye?'

A married couple are invited to a masked Halloween Party. She gets a terrible headache and tells her husband to go to the party alone. She takes an aspirin and goes to bed. He picks up his costume and goes to the party. The wife, after sleeping soundly for an hour, wakes up without any pain and decides to go to the party after all. As her husband has not seen her costume, she decides to have some fun by watching him to see how he acts when she is not with him. She joins the party and soon spots her husband cavorting around the room, dancing, it seems to her, with all the available talent in the room. She thinks she will play him at his own game, so she sidles up to him seductively. It being her husband, she comes on really strong, making various suggestive comments to him, in a disguised voice. Before too long they leave the party and make love in her car. Just before the traditional unmasking at midnight, she slips away, returns home, puts her costume away and goes to bed, wondering what kind of explanation he will make for his behaviour. She is sitting up, reading, when he comes in, and she asks what kind of time he had. 'Oh, pretty boring,' he says, 'It's never much fun when you're not there.' 'Did you dance much?' she asks. 'Not a single dance,' he replies. 'When I got there, I met Bob, Mike and Roy so we went into a bedroom and played cards all night. But you'll never believe what happened to the randy sod I loaned my costume to ... !'

A boy asked his dad, 'Did you know that in some parts of Africa, a man doesn't know his wife until he marries her?' His father replied, 'Why single out Africa?'

Emma said she will treat me like a pagan god, and I expect she will. Every evening, at dinner time, she'll probably bring me a burnt offering.

Poor old Richard sent his photograph off to a Lonely Hearts Club. They sent it back, saying they weren't that lonely.

In a recent survey, 70% of women thought their bum was too fat, 20% said their bum was too thin, and the other 10% said they didn't care ... they would have married him anyway.

A husband should forget his mistakes. There's no point in two people remembering the same things.

After just a few years of marriage, filled with constant arguments, the young couple decided the only way to save their relationship was to try counselling. The counsellor jumped right in and opened the floor for discussion. 'What seems to be the problem?' he asked. Faced with this direct approach, the husband stared out of the window, and remained silent. On the other hand, the wife began talking at 100 mph, describing all the wrongs in their marriage. After patiently listening to this tirade for over ten minutes, the counsellor eventually stood up, walked across the room, picked up the woman by her shoulders, kissed her passionately for several minutes and then sat her back down. She was speechless. Returning to his desk, the counsellor said to the disbelieving husband, 'Your wife needs that at least twice a week!' The husband scratched his head and replied, 'I can get her here every Monday and Wednesday.'

The smallest things seem to upset Jane. The other day she was doing a crossword puzzle and she asked me, 'What is a female sheep?' I said, 'Ewe,' and she burst into tears.

I'm so looking forward to coming home from work, opening a beer, sitting on the sofa and spending the evening watching Paula's favourite television programmes.

A husband and wife are at a dinner party, talking to some friends, when the subject of marriage counselling crops up. 'Oh, we'll never need that. My husband and I have a great relationship,' the wife explains, 'He's a communications consultant and I'm an actress. He talks really well to me, and I pretend to listen.'

Len's the kind of lad girls dream about. That's much better for them than seeing him in broad daylight.

During the wedding rehearsal, the groom approaches the vicar with an unusual offer. 'Look,' he says, 'I'll give you £100 if you change my wedding vows. It's easy money for you.

Just leave out the promise to love, honour and obey bit.' He gives the vicar £100 and walks away feeling very pleased with himself. On the wedding day, when the vows are exchanged, the vicar looks at the groom and says,' Do you promise to obey her every command and wish, serve her with breakfast in bed every morning and agree not to even look at another woman, as long as you both shall live?' The groom gulps, looks around in disbelief and horror, and says in a tiny voice, 'I do.' At the end of the service the groom approaches the vicar and says, 'I thought we had a deal.' The vicar places the £100 back in his hand and says, 'She made me a better offer.'

The first morning after their honeymoon, the husband gets up early, goes down to the kitchen, and brings his wife her breakfast in bed. Naturally, she is delighted. 'Have you noticed how lightly I have fried the egg and how crisply I have made the bacon?' he asks. 'Of course, dear,' she replies. 'That's good,' he says, 'because that's how I want my breakfast served every morning.'

A friend tells Joe that he got a set of golf clubs for his girlfriend, and Joe replies that he wishes he could make trade like that.

A man tells his friend, 'I married Miss Right – but I didn't know her first name was Always.'

May our only ups and downs be between the sheets.

Stan was chatting up this girl in the park, and he said, 'Will you come out for a meal with me tonight?' 'Oh no,' she replied, 'I never go out with perfect strangers.' And Stan replied, 'Who says I'm perfect?'

My best man could marry anyone he pleases. Problem is, he can't seem to please anyone.

In Bristol, people learn about life at a young age. Two five-year-olds were playing in the street when they saw a school friend peering through the window of a house. 'Quick. Come and see!' said the friend, 'There's a man fighting with a woman in bed.' One of the boys looked in, and said, 'They're not fighting, they're making love.' The third little boy took a quick glance, and said, 'Yes ... and badly.'

A man took his pregnant wife to the hospital to give birth, and the doctor told them, ' We've developed a new machine which you might like to try. It will take some of the pain of childbirth from the mother and give it to the father.' The doctor warned the man that he might find the pain unbearable, but they agreed to use the machine and set it at 10% to begin with. The man was surprised at how little pain he was experiencing and asked the doctor to raise it. So it went up to 20%. As he felt so unaffected he asked for it to go up to 50%, and finally 100%. 'Childbirth is easy,' the man thought to himself. After the baby was born, the man, woman and new baby all went home – only to hear that their postman had mysteriously died.

One night a newly married couple are watching television, when the wife decides to make herself a snack. As she approaches the kitchen, she sees a stranger eating some of her home-made cake. Quietly, she returns to the living room. She whispers to her husband, 'There's a burglar in the house, and he's eating my cake.' The husband replies, 'So should I call the police or an ambulance?'

'What do you love most about me?' a husband asks his wife. 'Is it my good looks or my superior intellect?' His wife replies, 'What I love about you most is your enormous sense of humour.'

A woman accompanies her husband to the doctor's surgery. After his check-up, the doctor calls the woman into his office alone. He says, 'Your husband is suffering from a very serious disease. If you don't do the following, your husband will surely die. Each morning, give him a healthy breakfast, be pleasant and make sure he is in a good mood. For lunch and dinner, make him a nutritious meal and don't discuss your problems with him because that would only make his stress worse. Most importantly of all,' the doctor continues, 'make love with your husband several times a week and satisfy his every whim. If you can do this for the next six months, I think your husband will regain his health completely.' On the way home, the husband asks his wife, 'What did the doctor say?' And she replies, 'You're going to die.'

I asked Eleanor's father if I could marry her, and he said, 'Just leave your name and phone number and we'll be in contact if nothing better comes up.'

On their first wedding anniversary, a husband says, 'Let's go out tonight and have some fun.' His wife replies, 'Great idea! But if you get back before I do, please leave the light on.'

They say marriage is a continuous process of getting used to things you hadn't expected.

Sally says we're to be equal partners in our marriage ... and I'm to be the silent one.

A woman tells her friend, 'My husband has developed a strange sexual practice recently. He insists on throwing me on the table and making love to me after we've finished eating.' 'That's not so strange,' her friend says. 'Oh, no?' replies the woman. 'Try explaining that to the manager of our local McDonalds.'

After a few months of marriage, a husband says, 'Truthfully, dear, you're too cold in bed. You don't do anything, you just lie there. Why don't you moan and groan passionately?' That night, as they are making love, she decides to heed his words of advice and begins to moan and groan with feeling. 'Oh, Martin, darling,' she begins, 'I had the most horrible day. The washing machine broke down, the rent man called, I burnt the cakes ... !'

I told Amy that since we'd met I hadn't been able to eat or drink. She asked, 'Is that because you love me so much?' 'No,' I replied, 'it's because I'm broke.'

A woman says to her husband, 'There's trouble with the car. It's got water in the carburettor.' 'Water in the carburettor? That's ridiculous,' he exclaims. But the woman insists, 'I tell you, there's water in the carburettor.' 'Darling,' he says, 'you don't even know what a carburettor is. Where's the car?' And the woman replies, 'In the river.'

We first met in a revolving door five years ago. And we've been going round together ever since.

A woman asks her friend, 'Is your husband a bookworm?' 'No, just a worm,' comes the reply.

A newlywed wife proudly announces to her husband, 'I made this pudding all by myself'. Her husband replies, 'Well done! But who helped you lift it out of the oven?'

A man places this ad in the local newspaper: For sale – Complete set of Encyclopaedia Britannica. £200 or nearest offer. No longer needed. Got married last week. Wife knows everything.

I said to Mr Phillips, 'I would like to have your daughter for my wife.' And he replied, 'Why, what would your wife want her for?'

Tim's looking for a wife. Trouble is, he can't find a woman who loves him as much as he loves himself.

A man has a terrible accident at work and his dangley bits get horribly mangled in a machine. He is rushed to hospital, where the doctor reassures him that modern medicine makes it possible for his appendage to be rebuilt, but this can only be done privately. The doctor tells him there are three choices: a small one can be built for £2000, a medium one for £4000, or a large one for £6000. The doctor suggests that since the decision affects both the man and his wife, he should discuss it with her privately before making the final decision. The doctor leaves the A&E department and, while he is gone, the man phones his wife to explain the options available. The doctor returns and finds the man looking very depressed. 'Were you and your wife able to reach a decision?' the doctor asks. 'Yes,' says the man, 'after carefully examining all the options, my wife decided that she would rather have a new fitted kitchen.'

Before we got engaged, I asked Anne, 'If we get married, do you think you'll be able to live on my income?' Anne replied, 'Of course, dear. But what will you live on?'

Mrs Brown and her little daughter Emily are outside the church, watching all the comings and goings at a wedding. After all the photographs have been taken and everyone has driven off to the reception, Emily asks her mother, 'Mummy, why did the bride change her mind?' 'What do you mean, change her mind?' her mum replies. 'Well,' says Emily, 'she went in with one man and came out with another.'

A newly married bride says to her husband, 'Darling, don't expect the first few meals to be great. It takes time to find a good take-away.'

As the train stood at the station, a man asks the guard, 'Do I have time to say goodbye to my wife?' 'That depends, sir,' replies the guard, 'How long have you been married?'

A young Italian girl finally marries her beau. They do not have enough money for a honeymoon away, so the mother of the bride lets them stay at her home. The young bride, a virgin, is very nervous about spending her first night with her husband. When the time comes, he takes off his shirt, revealing a hairy chest. The young bride gasps and runs down to her mother. She cries, 'Momma! He has hair all over his chest!' Her mother looks up at her and says, 'Don't worry, my daughter, all good Italian men have hairy chests. Run back upstairs and take good care of him.' The bride goes back to the room, as her husband is taking off his trousers, revealing his hairy legs. She runs to her mother and cries, 'Momma! He has hairy legs!' The mother looks up at her daughter and says, 'Don't worry, my daughter, all good Italian men have hairy legs. Run back upstairs and take good care of him.' The bride goes back to the room, as her husband is taking off his socks. One foot is perfectly formed but half of the other one is missing. She runs back to her mother and screams, 'Momma! He has a foot and a half!' The mother looks up at her daughter, pushes her out of the way, and says, 'Stay here, my daughter, this is a job for Momma!'

A husband-to-be is telling all his friends he is going to marry the most faithful, trustworthy and loyal girl in the world, when his prospective brother-in-law interrupts him, saying, 'What a shame! And after all the time you've been engaged to my little sister!'

A man says to his friend, 'I was hypnotised last week.' The friend asks, 'What does hypnotised mean?' The man replies, 'Why to hypnotise is to get a man in your power, and make him do whatever you want.' The friend says, 'That's not hypnotism, that's marriage.'

George does an eight hour working day, and he makes sure he gets eight hours sleep. Problem is, they're always the same eight hours.

A girl asks her boyfriend to come over that evening to have dinner with her parents. She tells him that after the meal her parents will be going out to a show, so they will be alone. Thinking his luck may be in, the boy goes to the chemist to buy a pack-of-three. He is rather nervous about making his purchase, but the chemist is very understanding and eventually the boy leaves the shop with his condoms. That evening, the boy turns up at the girl's parents' house and meets his girlfriend at the door. 'Oh, I'm so excited for you to meet my parents,' she says, 'Come on in!' The boy goes inside and is taken to the dinner table where the girl's parents are already seated. The boy immediately offers to say grace and bows his head. Time passes and the boy continues to look to the floor. Finally, the girl leans over and whispers to her boyfriend, 'I had no idea you were so religious.' To which her boyfriend responds, 'And I had no idea your father was a chemist!'

A newlywed wife asks her husband, 'Will you love me when I'm old, fat and ugly?' Her husband replies, 'Of course I do!'

Roy's ambition is to marry a rich girl who is too proud to let her husband work.

A month or so after their wedding, Tina says to her mother, 'Mum, we had a dreadful fight last night!' Her mum replies, 'Don't worry, dear. Every marriage must have it's first fight.' 'I know! I know!' says Tina, 'But what shall I do with the body?'

After a couple had been married for about a year, the wife dislocates her jaw. The husband calls the doctor and says,

'Doctor, I'm phoning on behalf of my wife because she's had an accident and can't speak. Can she make an appointment to see you ... in about three or four months time?'

I told Lucy, 'Now we're married, I want you to stick to your washing, ironing, cooking, cleaning and shopping ... No wife of mine is going to work!'

A newlywed husband is acting as an usher during the Sunday morning service at the Church of St Jude. His bride is in the congregation. Becoming terribly worried about having left the roast in the oven, she writes a note to her husband, sending it to him via another usher. This second usher, thinking it is a note for the vicar, hurries down the aisle and lays it on the pulpit. Stopping abruptly in the middle of his sermon to read the note, the astonished vicar is met with this written instruction: 'Please go home immediately and turn off the gas.'

Problems in marriage frequently arise because a man too often shows his worse side to his better half.

I'm told a man really knows he's married when his wife puts one dent in his bank account and another in his car.

An engaged man asks his friend how he could find out whether his bride-to-be really is totally sexually inexperienced, as she claims to be. And his mate replies, 'All you need is some red paint, some blue paint, and a spade. Paint one ball red and one ball blue. Then, on your honeymoon, if she laughs and says, "Those are the funniest balls I've ever seen", you hit her with the spade.'

A woman says to her friend, 'I hear you've got a new dishwasher.' And her friend replies, 'Yes, I got married again.'

At bedtime, an amorous husband prepares two aspirins and a glass of water for his wife. 'What's that for?' she asks. 'For your headache, dear,' he replies. 'But I don't have a headache,' she insists. 'Then tonight's the night!' he exclaims.

When Mr and Mrs Henry Ford celebrated their golden wedding anniversary, a reporter asked Henry, 'To what do you attribute your fifty years of successful married life?' 'The formula,' he replied, 'is the same formula I have always used in making cars – just stick to one model.'

A newlywed couple are spending their honeymoon in an isolated log cabin in the Scottish Highlands. They had registered with the cabin's owner, an elderly farmer, a week earlier and had not been seen since. Becoming increasingly concerned about their well-being, the old man decides to go and see if they are alright. He knocks on the door of the cabin and a weak voice from inside answers, 'Yes, we're fine. We're living off the fruits of love.' And the old chap says, 'I thought so. Would you mind not throwing the peelings out of the window. They're choking my ducks.'

A young man gets on his knees and says, 'I'm not rich like Russell, and I don't have a country estate like James or a Porsche like Billy ... but I love you and want to marry you.' And the girl replies, 'I love you too, but what did you say about James?'

A newlywed bride proudly announces to her friend, 'I cooked my first meal last night ... and it was a great success.' 'I'm so pleased,' her friend replies. And the newlywed continues, 'Yes, my husband says we're going out for meals every night from now on.'

Dave is loudly lamenting to everyone in the pub that his doctor has ordered him to give up half of his sex life. 'Which half are you going to give up?' asks a bored listener. 'Talking about it or thinking about it?'

Bob's clothes never go out of style. They look just as old-fashioned every year.

A salesman is trying to persuade a housewife to take out a life assurance policy on her husband. 'Just imagine, if your husband were to die,' he says, 'What would you get?' 'Oh, a King Charles spaniel, I think,' she replies. 'They're so well-behaved.'

Maybe you've heard about the man whose credit card was stolen but decided not to report it because the thief was spending less than his wife did.

Just imagine, if it weren't for marriage, men would go through life thinking they had no faults at all.

I've been told that no matter how often a married man changes his job, he still ends up with the same boss.

Phil just gave me this excellent piece of advice ... he said, Dave, whenever you have a discussion with your new wife, always remember to get the last two words in: 'Yes, dear!'

8   Sample Speeches

Finally, it's time to put it all together by taking a look at some full length speeches. While you may decide to adapt, personalise, and possibly combine what you consider to be the best bits, the main reason for including them in this final chapter is to remind you of the style and tone you should adopt throughout your speech. Your address should be emotional and optimistic, yet enlivened throughout with humour. It should also be *short*.

Each of the speeches that follow should take no more than five to ten minutes to deliver. Don't make the same mistake as the bridegroom who didn't have a stop button. He babbled on and on, oblivious to his increasingly restless audience. Finally, one of the more drunken guests hurled an empty champagne bottle at him. It missed, and hit his bride instead. As the bride slid slowly down the wall to the floor clutching her head, she was heard to mumur, 'Hit me again, hit me again ... I can still hear him.'

On the big day, don't hit the bottle, or you may have a limp excuse that night for not rising to the occasion ... But equally, don't risk the bottle hitting you, by rabbiting on and on at the reception!

Sample Speech 1

Reverend Green, Ladies and Gentlemen – Friends, we are told that marriage is a lottery. Well if it is, then I have hit the jackpot. Quite simply, I am the luckiest man in the world to have a wife like Karen and and to have friends like you to join us on this, our happiest day – happiest day so far that is. Most couples describe their wedding day as the happiest day of their lives. That worries me because it implies that as from tomorrow there's a lifelong decline ahead. That will not be the case with us. Karen, in the words of your favourite Carpenters' song, 'We've only just begun'. I love you more than yesterday, but less than tomorrow. Our love will continue to grow ... and grow!

You know, I've been lucky in so many ways. Lucky in having the best parents in the world. Parents who knew that the most important thing they could do for their children was to love each other. Lucky in my new parents-in-law. What a horrible expression that is – parents-in-law. Let's call them parents-by-marriage. Roy, on behalf of my wife and I, thank you for those kind words, and thanks to you and June for giving us such a lovely wedding and reception, and, even more, for producing a daughter like Karen.

And I really must thank you all for your presence – in both senses of the word. Karen and I are delighted that you all managed to come to our wedding and to have received all those generous gifts. I cannot begin to tell you how much they mean to us. But, once we've returned from the honeymoon, I'll see the guy at the pawn shop, and then I'll have a far better idea.

But let's face it, Karen is a very lucky lady, too. No, I don't mean because she married me, although I suppose she could have done worse. No, I mean because today she also gained two wonderful parents-by-marriage.

Thanks must also go to Ryan for being such an efficient best man. Although I'm not sure how thankful to be because I haven't heard his speech yet. As many of you know, before Ryan joined us at Sun Hill, he was a community cop at West Huntspill. It was early one morning when he received a phone call from an elderly man. 'I can't sleep for the noise,' he complained. 'What's causing it? Do you want me to make an arrest or seize their music equipment?' Ryan asked. 'I'm not sure. It's two cats mating on the wall outside my house. They're making a hideous racket with all their love-making and things.' 'Cats!' exclaimed Ryan. 'Why don't you walk up to the cats, give one of them a sharp prod and tell them that he is wanted on the phone?' 'Will that stop them?' the man asked. 'Well, it certainly stopped me,' Ryan replied bitterly ... Ryan, thank you so much for doing the business for me so well today. No one could hope for a better best man than you!

Now Karen, you thought you knew all the 'thank you's' that would be in my speech. Well there's one you didn't know about. I thank you for becoming my lovely bride. You can't help being lovely ... but you could help becoming my bride. Today, I married my best friend – the lady I laugh with, live for and dream with. Karen, in the words of Robert Browning: 'Grow old with me, the best is yet to be!'

Finally, our thanks must go to the delightful young ladies who have done such a great job in helping Karen up the aisle – although I hope she came to the church of her own free will. They have been wonderful and added so much to the occasion. So please join me in drinking a toast to Petunia, Iris, Primrose and Rose.

Ladies and Gentlemen, the bridesmaids!

Sample Speech 2

Ladies and Gentlemen, I have some good news and some bad news. First the bad news – after writing and re-writing, editing and re-editing, the very shortest I could make this speech is one hour and eighteen minutes. That was the bad news ... now for the good news – I was lying about the bad news.

So here we are ... we've done it ... we've tied the knot! And, quite simply, I'm the happiest man in the world. My wife and I are delighted that you could all make it to our wedding today. Thank you, James, for those wise words. As they say, better late than never. You see, we needed a few saucepans and a new toaster and as Argos was closed ... I do not deserve the good things you said of me, but I shall try so hard to deserve them and be worthy of Sarah.

I'd like to take this opportunity to say a few other thank-yous, too. I can't imagine a happier way to start married life than with our family and friends around us. So thank you all for being here. Whether you travelled two miles or two thousand – as Doug and Patsy did – you are all so very welcome. It wouldn't be the same without you. And thank you for all your generous gifts. I know Sarah will find the lawn mower and electric drill particularly useful, and I will certainly make good use of the garden hammock and the deck chairs.

I am also delighted to have James and Joyce as my new in-laws. When I asked James for Sarah's hand in marriage, he said to me, 'Mark, do you think you're earning enough money to support a family?' I said I thought I did. And James replied, 'Think very carefully now, lad. After all, there are six of us!' Only joking, James. I want you to know that I really do feel one of the family now.

They say a girl grows up to be like her mother. Well, I can only hope it's true. James, Joyce, you produced a beautiful, intelligent, kind, funny, caring ... Sorry, Sarah, I can't read your writing. What does this say, love? No, Sarah is beautiful and intelligent. I'll leave everyone here to decide which trait comes from which parent. And I never thought I could be as happy as I am today without City winning the Premiership. Sarah, I love you so much:

> 'I am yours, you are mine,
> Of this we are certain.
> You are locked in my heart,
> the small key is lost.
> You must stay forever.'

When I asked Sarah to marry me, I knew I would need a best man, and there was no doubt who that would be ... our tax-collecting friend, Ian. Despite his job, Ian really is almost human. In fact, I'll share a little secret with you ... he's a bit of a hero, on the quiet.

I hope I won't embarrass him by telling you all, but last summer a frantic-looking woman came rushing out of her house into the street, near Ian's office, and cried: 'Help! Help! My son has swallowed a coin and is choking. I don't know what to do!' People in the street all looked the other way, except one ... Ian. Ian rushed into the woman's house, found her young son, turned him upside down and shook him violently until the coin fell out of his mouth. 'Oh, thank you!' cried the woman in happiness. 'Are you a doctor?' 'No, love,' Ian replied, 'I'm with the Inland Revenue.'

I've almost finished, because this suit has to be back at Moss Bros in twenty minutes. So finally, I'd like to recite two other short poems, which, I believe, express the sometimes different, yet essentially complimentary views and attitudes of the two genders towards love, marriage and life. I hope, like me, you will find them uplifting, as they encapsulate the importance and true meaning of institution of marriage, and illustrate the respective priorities of the two genders. First an ode entitled Moods of a Woman:

'An ageless truth, a work of fiction,
A woman is a bundle of contradiction,
She is afraid of a wasp, will scream at a mouse,
Yet will tackle an intruder, alone in the house,
Smelling delightful, as sweet as a rose,
She'll kiss you one minute, then turn up her nose.
She'll win you in cotton, enchant you in silk,
She'll be stronger than brandy, yet weaker than milk,
At times she'll be vengeful, merry and sad,
She'll hate you like poison, and love you like mad.'

And now a short poem entitled Moods of a Man:

'Horny.'

Now it's time for another toast – any excuse for a drink. It's my final duty – no, pleasure, to thank the bridesmaids for helping Sarah up the aisle today. They all did their jobs magnificently. Please stand, raise your glasses and drink a toast to the bridesmaids . . .

The bridesmaids!

Sample Speech 3

Someone once said that a good speech has both a good beginning and a good ending. A great speech, however, keeps both of these very close together. I can't promise you a great speech, but I intend to make it a short one, because of my throat ... if I go on too long, Jayne has threatened to cut it!

I just want to thank Bill for those kind words. It's amazing what people will say when they're not under oath. No, I appreciate everything you have said and I promise I will take good care of Jayne. Think of it this way, Bill: you're not losing a daughter ... you're gaining a bathroom.

On behalf of Jayne and myself, I'd also like to thank everyone for joining us here today and for being so generous with your gifts. With all those saucepans and toasters, looks like we're going to have to get used to plenty of boiled toast.

I'm also delighted to have Angela and Bill as my second set of parents. I knew we'd hit it off when I fell in love with Jayne because they have helped her to become the lady she is – like me, fond of real ale and swimming. I learned to swim at a very early age. When I was three, my parents used to row me out to sea in a little boat until they got about a mile from the shore – then I had to swim back. I quite liked the swim – it was getting out of the bag that was difficult.

Just joking, Mum and Dad, although I have given you plenty of good reasons over the years for doing that. I'd really like to take this opportunity to say a huge thanks to you both. You should receive a medal for endurance. You loved and supported me through every stage of my life, including my Bart Simpson years, that seemed to extend well into my 20's. Jayne may argue that they are by no means over yet. Mum and Dad, thanks for your contribution to today's festivities and for teaching me the difference between right and wrong, so I know which I'm enjoying at any particular time.

I hear that Dad gave Jayne a receipt this afternoon. It reads: 'Delivered, one son as promised, sold as seen, no refunds under any circumstances. We've redecorated the room and changed the locks, so you're stuck with him. Dehydrates easily, top up with beer regularly.'

Now for the emotional bit. Emotional and 100% genuine. Jayne, I love you. Thank you for making me the happiest man in the world. Someone once said, 'When you love someone, everything is clear – where to go, what to do – it all takes care of itself, and you don't have to ask anyone about anything.' That's exactly how I feel here today. When I asked a few of you earlier what Jayne looked like today, you all told me she looked wonderful, but this didn't prepare me for the sight I got when I turned round in the church to see her myself. You look gorgeous, darling. Marriage is our last, best chance to grow up. Today I grew up.

And what about my dashing best man? You did a great job today. Thank you, Greg, for being the perfect best man. But where's your duck today? Is it with you? ... Greg has a pet duck and he usually takes it with him everywhere he goes. Last week he was most upset because, although he bought two tickets, the duck was refused admission to the theatre. So he decided to stuff the duck down his trousers and pretend to be a little overweight. The ruse worked, and Greg got in to see the show. Everything went well until the intermission when the duck got very hot and poked his beak out of Greg's trousers, through his flies. Two old ladies were sitting next to him and one nudged the other and whispered, 'Look at this.' The other lady said, 'I can't stop looking at it ... it's eating my ice cream!' Ladies, Greg is looking a little overweight again today, so I'd be very careful if you find yourself sitting next to him.

Finally, my wife and I would like to say a special thanks to the charming bridesmaids, Charlotte, Emily and Ann. They have been wonderful. In fact, I think we should drink a toast to them, don't you?

Ladies and Gentlemen, the bridesmaids!

A Final Word

The final word is really yours, of course, because this handbook has been no more than a motorist's manual. Precisely how and where you drive is up to you. You will say the most important words of the day, if not your life, when you say, 'I do'. Your speech gives you an unparalleled opportunity to follow this up by thanking everybody involved and by telling your bride publicly how much you love her.

Now it's time for me to take a back seat and for you to take the wheel. I wish you a safe, enjoyable and memorable journey!